Cursive Writing

Instruction, Practice, and Reinforcement

Authors: Schyrlet Cameron and Carolyn Craig
Editor: Mary Dieterich
Proofreader: Margaret Brown

COPYRIGHT © 2018 Mark Twain Media, Inc.

ISBN 978-1-62223-700-5

Printing No. CD-405023

Mark Twain Media, Inc., Publishers
Distributed by Carson-Dellosa Publishing LLC

Visit us at www.carsondellosa.com

Table of Contents

To the Teacher

For several years, there has been a push to drop cursive writing instruction from the middle-school grades and instead concentrate solely on keyboarding skills. Recently, educators have realized success in the 21st century requires students to be fluent in both handwriting and keyboarding. As of 2016, seventeen states have set standards for "Written Language Production."

Cursive Writing: Instruction, Practice, and Reinforcement is designed to be an effective, easy-to-use resource for teachers and parents. This book provides instruction that demonstrates proper letter formation, practice in writing individual letters and letter combinations, reinforcement in word and sentence writing, and enrichment activities. This book includes:

- tips for posture, paper position, and pencil grip

- pre- and post-assessment

- cursive writing rubric

- annotated letter formation with numbered arrows that demonstrate the sequence and direction of strokes

- trace and write exercises

- supported practice with examples of letter formation

- practice writing sentences and paragraphs in cursive

- copy work practice with reproduction of the letters from memory

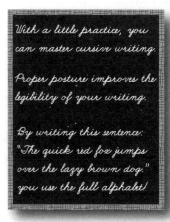

Cursive Writing: Instruction, Practice, and Reinforcement can be utilized as a unit of instruction. The lessons also can be used independently or combined with others to review and reinforce skills targeted for improvement. The book can be used as supplemental material to enhance the middle-school curriculum in the classroom, for independent study, or as a tutorial at home.

This book presents one style of cursive writing. It is a fairly simple style without much added flourish to the letters. There are many different styles used in instructional materials, and students will develop their own style of handwriting as they practice and mature. This book presents a basic style for those who have never learned cursive writing and for those who need more practice to improve their penmanship. If there are students who have learned different methods for forming certain letters, it is suggested that they not be penalized for using those methods, as long as the letters are legible and flow well with the writing samples.

Due to the limitations of the cursive font software used in this book, some letter connections are not always made smoothly and completely. Every effort has been made to complete the letter connections and indicate how the text should look in actual cursive writing.

Penmanship and the Middle-School Grades

What Is Penmanship?
Penmanship is the method of writing with the hand using a writing instrument, such as a pen or pencil.

What Is Cursive Writing?
Cursive writing, also known as longhand, is a form of penmanship. Letters are written joined together in a flowing manner.

Why Teach Cursive Writing?
For several years, instruction in cursive handwriting has been limited or dropped altogether from the school curriculum. Recently, parents and teachers have come to realize there are benefits to learning cursive writing skills. Being able to read and write cursive allows students to:
- read teachers' written assignments.
- read teachers' comments on their graded work.
- read historical documents.
- become quick note-takers.
- write their personal signature.

Take It Back to the Basics
1. Writing Portfolio: A writing folder will allow each student to collect and organize their completed worksheets, evaluations, and projects.

2. 3 P's of Penmanship: The correct posture, paper placement, and pencil grip is important to producing legible handwriting. The tripod grasp method is the best way to hold a pencil, for both right- and left-handed writers. But by middle school, many students may have learned a different style. We do not advise trying to change a functional adapted grip, but instead try to improve the grip if possible.

3. Pre- and Post-Assessment: Evaluate individual student accuracy in cursive writing before beginning instruction. The results can be used to determine if students need instruction, practice, or review to improve their current handwriting skills.

4. Instruction: Teaching correct letter formation and letter connection is basic to students developing good handwriting habits. This book contains worksheets demonstrating these skills, but modeling by the teacher is also useful. It is important to note that handwriting style is unique to each student. Allowances should be made for a student's personal style while stressing legibility.

5. Practice: The key to successfully improving penmanship is practice, practice, and more practice. Worksheets from this book can be copied and distributed to students to complete while the teacher is taking roll, collecting homework, or conferencing with individual students.

6. Enrichment: Find reasons for students to use their cursive writing skills: journaling, writing to a pen pal, or designing and creating personalized stationary and note cards.

The 3 P's of Cursive Writing

Posture

The proper body position will improve the legibility of your writing. You should sit straight in the chair with feet on the floor. Lean forward slightly, and place both arms on the desk top.

Paper

The proper letter slant is achieved by correctly positioning your handwriting paper on the desk top. Place your paper at an angle.

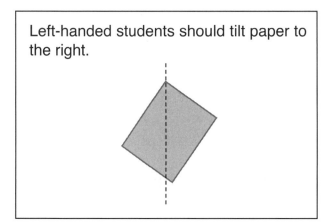

Left-handed students should tilt paper to the right.

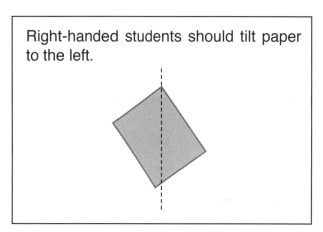

Right-handed students should tilt paper to the left.

Pencil

The proper pencil grip allows you to write neatly at a reasonable speed without putting a strain on your hand. The tripod pencil grip is the most common way to hold a pencil, for both left- and right-handed writers.

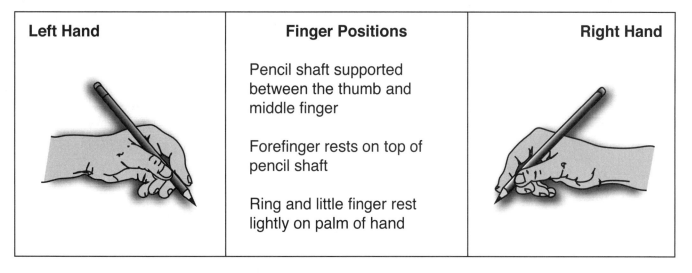

Left Hand	Finger Positions	Right Hand
	Pencil shaft supported between the thumb and middle finger Forefinger rests on top of pencil shaft Ring and little finger rest lightly on palm of hand	

　　　　　3

Name: _____ Date: _____

Cursive Writing Assessment

Part 1: Forming Uppercase and Lowercase Letters

Directions: The letters of the alphabet are printed below. Now, you write the uppercase and lowercase letters in cursive writing.

A a

I i

B b

J j

C c

K k

D d

L l

E e

M m

F f

N n

G g

O o

H h

P p

Name: _____ Date: _____

Cursive Writing Assessment (cont.)

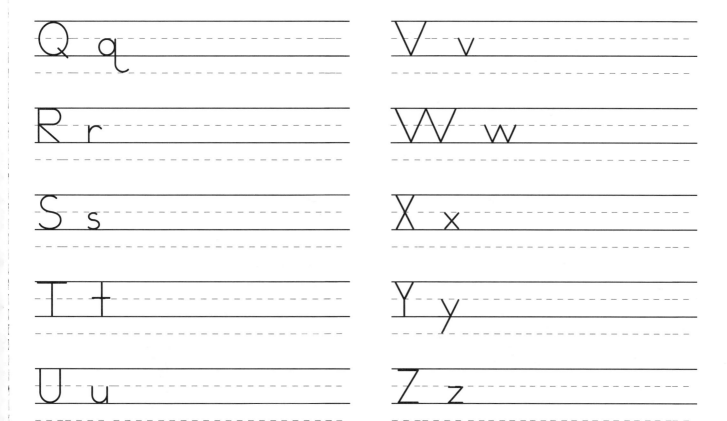

Part 2: Forming and Connecting Letters

Directions: Write the sentence in cursive writing.

The quick brown fox jumped over the lazy dog.

Name: _____ Date: _____

Cursive Writing Rubric

Part 1: Forming Uppercase and Lowercase Letters					
Criteria	Excellent 4	Good 3	Fair 2	Poor 1	Score
Letter Formation	Letters are correctly formed.	Most of the letters are formed correctly.	Many letters are not formed correctly.	Few letters are formed correctly.	
Letter Size	All letter size is appropriate for the line space.	Most letter size is appropriate for the line space.	Many examples of incorrect letter size.	Letter size not appropriate for line space (too small or too large).	
Letter Slant	All letters have a uniform slant.	Most letters have a uniform slant.	Many letters do not have a uniform slant.	Slant of letters varies from letter to letter.	
Part 2: Forming and Connecting Letters					
Criteria	Excellent 4	Good 3	Fair 2	Poor 1	Score
Legibility	Writing is of superior quality.	Writing is legible.	Writing is partially legible.	Writing is difficult to read.	
Forming and Connecting Letters	All letters are correctly formed and connected correctly.	Most letters are correctly formed and connected correctly.	Many letters are not correctly formed or connected correctly.	Few letters are correctly formed and connected correctly.	
Spacing	Spacing is uniform between letters and words.	Most spacing is uniform between letters and words.	Many examples of uneven spacing between letters and words.	Spacing is inconsistent between letters and words.	

Teacher Comments:

Name: _____

Date: _____

Cursive Letter Guide

Directions: The chart below can be used to review the correct formation of uppercase and lowercase letters, numbers, and punctuation marks. Place the chart in your writing folder.

Uppercase Letters

Lowercase Letters

Numbers and Punctuation Marks

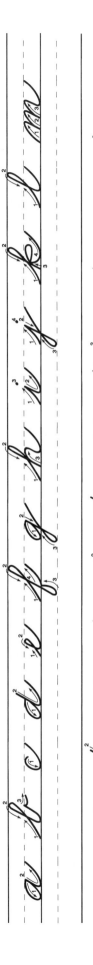

Practice Paper

Name: _____ Date: _____

Cursive Guided Practice

Ɑ a Ɑ a

Directions: Trace the line of dotted letters. Then practice writing the uppercase or lowercase letters that follow.

a a a a a a a a

a

a

a a a a a a a a a

a

a

Aa

Name: _____ Date: _____

Cursive Guided Practice

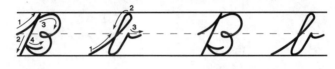

Directions: Trace the line of dotted letters. Then practice writing the upper or lowercase letters that follow.

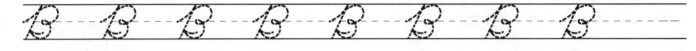

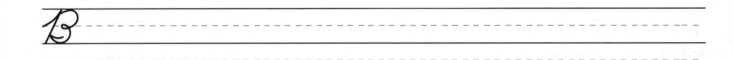

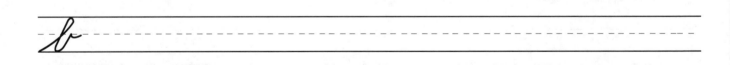

Name: _____ Date: _____

Cursive Guided Practice

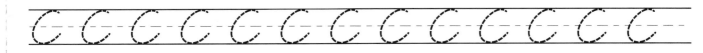

Directions: Trace the line of dotted letters. Then practice writing the uppercase or lowercase letters that follow.

Name: _____ Date: _____

Cursive Guided Practice

D d D d

Directions: Trace the line of dotted letters. Then practice writing the uppercase or lowercase letters that follow.

Name: _____ Date: _____

Cursive Guided Practice

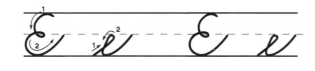

Directions: Trace the line of dotted letters. Then practice writing the uppercase or lowercase letters that follow.

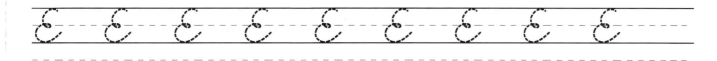

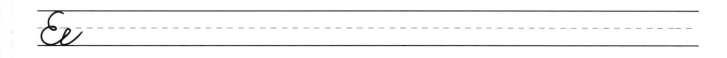

Cursive Guided Practice

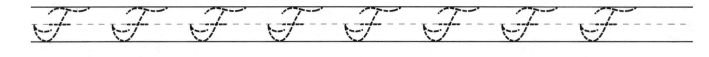

Directions: Trace the line of dotted letters. Then practice writing the uppercase and lowercase letters that follow.

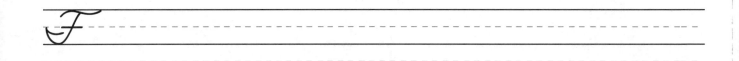

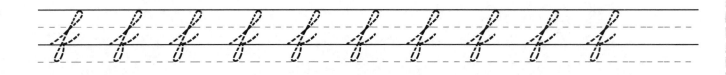

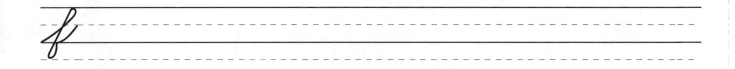

Name: _____ Date: _____

Cursive Guided Practice

Directions: Trace the line of dotted letters. Then practice writing the uppercase or lowercase letters that follow.

Name: _____ Date: _____

Cursive Guided Practice

Directions: Trace the line of dotted letters. Then practice writing the uppercase or lowercase letters that follow.

Name: _____ Date: _____

Cursive Guided Practice

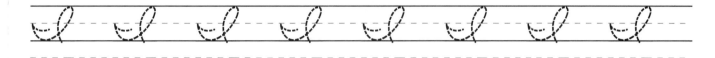

Directions: Trace the line of dotted letters. Then practice writing the uppercase or lowercase letters that follow.

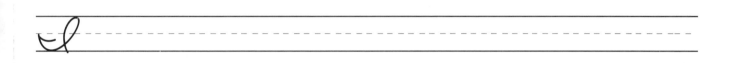

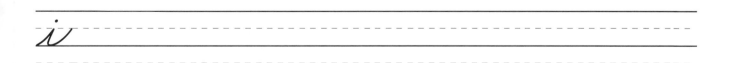

Name: _____ Date: _____

Cursive Guided Practice

Directions: Trace the line of dotted letters. Then practice writing the uppercase and lowercase letters that follow.

Name: _____ Date: _____

Cursive Guided Practice

Directions: Trace the line of dotted letters. Then practice writing the uppercase or lowercase letters that follow.

Name: _____ Date: _____

Cursive Guided Practice

Directions: Trace the line of dotted letters. Then practice writing the uppercase and lowercase letters.

Name: _____ Date: _____

Cursive Guided Practice

M m M m

Directions: Trace the line of dotted letters. Then practice writing the uppercase or lowercase letters that follow.

m m m m m m m m

m

m

m m m m m m m

m

m

Mm

Name: _____ Date: _____

Cursive Guided Practice

n m n m

Directions: Trace the line of dotted letters. Then practice writing the uppercase and lowercase letters that follow.

Name: _____ Date: _____

Cursive Guided Practice

Directions: Trace the line of dotted letters. Then practice writing the uppercase or lowercase letters that follow.

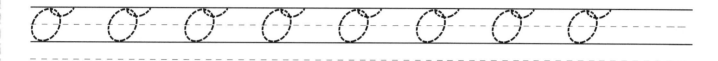

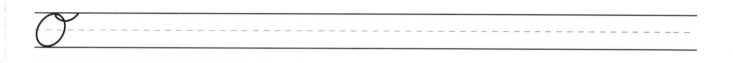

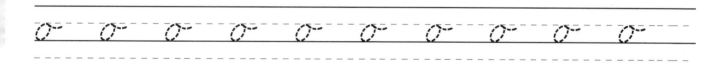

Name: _____ Date: _____

Cursive Guided Practice

Directions: Trace the line of dotted letters. Then practice writing the uppercase and lowercase letters that follow.

Name: _____ Date: _____

Cursive Guided Practice

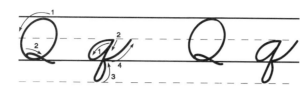

Directions: Trace the line of dotted letters. Then practice writing the uppercase or lowercase letters that follow.

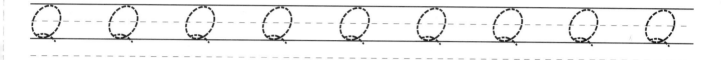

Name: _____ Date: _____

Cursive Guided Practice

Directions: Trace the line of dotted letters. Then practice writing the uppercase or lowercase letters that follow.

Name: _____ Date: _____

Cursive Guided Practice

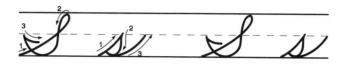

Directions: Trace the line of dotted letters. Then practice writing the uppercase or lowercase letters that follow.

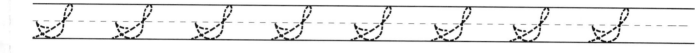

Name: _____ Date: _____

Cursive Guided Practice

Directions: Trace the line of dotted letters. Then practice writing the uppercase or lowercase letters that follow.

Name: _____ Date: _____

Cursive Guided Practice

$\mathcal{U} \quad \mathcal{u} \quad \mathcal{U} \quad \mathcal{u}$

Directions: Trace the line of dotted letters. Then practice writing the uppercase or lowercase letters that follow.

$\mathcal{U} \quad \mathcal{U} \quad \mathcal{U} \quad \mathcal{U} \quad \mathcal{U} \quad \mathcal{U} \quad \mathcal{U} \quad \mathcal{U}$

$\mathcal{U}$

$\mathcal{U}$

$\mathcal{u} \quad \mathcal{u} \quad \mathcal{u} \quad \mathcal{u} \quad \mathcal{u} \quad \mathcal{u} \quad \mathcal{u} \quad \mathcal{u}$

$\mathcal{u}$

$\mathcal{u}$

$\mathcal{Uu}$

Name: _____ Date: _____

Cursive Guided Practice

Directions: Trace the line of dotted letters. Then practice writing the uppercase and lowercase letters that follow.

Name: _____ Date: _____

Cursive Guided Practice

Directions: Trace the line of dotted letters. Then practice writing the uppercase or lowercase letters that follow.

Name: _____ Date: _____

Cursive Guided Practice

Directions: Trace the line of dotted letters. Then practice writing the uppercase or lowercase letters that follow.

Name: _____ Date: _____

Cursive Guided Practice

Yy Yy Yy Yy

Directions: Trace the line of dotted letters. Then practice writing the uppercase or lowercase letters that follow.

Y Y Y Y Y Y Y Y Y Y Y Y Y

Y

Y

Y Y Y Y Y Y Y Y Y

y

y

Yy

Name: _____ Date: _____

Cursive Guided Practice

Directions: Trace the line of dotted letters. Then practice writing the uppercase or lowercase letters that follow.

Name: _____   Date: _____

Practice Numbers and Punctuation Marks

Directions: Practice writing the numbers and punctuation marks.

1

2

3

4

5

6

7

8

9

? /

Name: _____ Date: _____

Letter Combinations: a, c, d, g, o, q

Directions: Practice writing the letter and letter groups after each example.

a   *aa*   *aaa*

c   *cc*   *ccc*

d   *dd*   *ddd*

g   *gg*   *ggg*

o   *oo*   *ooo*

q   *qq*   *qqq*

go   *do*   *dog*

cog   *add*

dad   *good*

goad   *quad*

Name: _____ Date: _____

Letter combinations: r, s, u, v, w

Directions: Practice writing the letter and letter groups after each example.

r　　　　*rr*　　　　*rrr*

s　　　　*ss*　　　　*sss*

u　　　　*uuu*　　　　*uuuu*

v　　　　*vv*　　　　*vvv*

w　　　　*wvw*　　　　*wvwvw*

so　　　　*we*

rat　　　　*vow*

cut　　　　*use*

saw　　　　*rib*

were　　　　*vote*

Name: _____ Date: _____

Letter Combinations: i, j, p, t

Directions: Practice writing the letter and letter groups after each example.

i   *ii*   *iii*

j   *jj*   *jjj*

p   *pp*   *ppp*

t   *tt*   *ttt*

it   *pit*

jig   *jog*

cop   *dig*

top   *pig*

paid   *gait*

toad   *join*

Name: _____ Date: _____

Letter Combinations: e, b, f, h, k, l

Directions: Practice writing the letter and letter groups after each example.

e   *ee*   *eee*

b   *bb*   *bbb*

f   *ff*   *fff*

h   *hh*   *hhh*

k   *kk*   *kkk*

l   *ll*   *lll*

be   *he*   *belt*

elf   *let*

help   *keep*

flee   *beak*

Name: _____ Date: _____

Letter combinations: m, n, x, y, z

Directions: Practice writing the letter and letter groups after each example.

m   *mm*   *mmm*

n   *nn*   *nnn*

x   *xx*   *xxx*

y   *yy*   *yyy*

z   *zz*   *zzz*

no   *in*

mow   *yam*

may   *mix*

next   *zinc*

yard   *zero*

Name: _____ Date: _____

Days of the Week and Abbreviations

Directions: Practice writing the days of the week.

Sunday

Monday

Tuesday

Wednesday

Thursday

Friday

Saturday

Sun.   *Mon.*

Tues.   *Wed.*

Thurs.   *Fri.*

Sat.

Name: _____ Date: _____

Months of the Year

Directions: Practice writing the months of the year.

January

February

March

April

May

June

July

August

September

October

November

December

Name: _____ Date: _____

Common Abbreviations

Directions: Practice writing these common abbreviations. Don't forget the period.

Apt.   *mgr.*

Ln.   *qt.*

Ste.   *sq.*

ext.   *tsp.*

lb.   *Gov.*

ft.   *Hwy.*

Dr.   *in.*

pt.   *min.*

doz.   *adj.*

Rd.   *Capt.*

Name: _____ Date: _____

Historical Document: Declaration of Independence

We hold these truths to be self-evident, that all men are created equal, that they are endowed by their Creator with certain unalienable Rights, that among these are Life, Liberty and the pursuit of Happiness.

Directions: Copy the excerpt using proper cursive writing form.

_____

_____

_____

_____

_____

_____

_____

Name: _____ Date: _____

Historical Document: Preamble to the U. S. Constitution

We the People of the United States, in order to form a more perfect Union, establish Justice, insure domestic Tranquility, provide for the common defence, promote the general Welfare, and secure the Blessings of Liberty to ourselves and our Posterity, do ordain and establish this Constitution for the United States of America.

Directions: Copy the excerpt using proper cursive writing form.

_____

_____

_____

_____

_____

_____

_____

_____

_____

Name: _____ Date: _____

Historical Document: Gettysburg Address

Four score and seven years ago our fathers brought forth, upon this continent, a new nation, conceived in liberty, and dedicated to the proposition that all men are created equal.

Directions: Copy the excerpt using proper cursive writing form.

Name: _____ Date: _____

Famous Quotes of the American Revolution

Directions: Copy the quotes using proper cursive writing form.

"These are the times that try men's souls."

--Thomas Paine

_____
- -
_____
- -
_____

"I know not what course others may take; but as for me, give me liberty or give me death!"

--Patrick Henry

_____
- -
_____
- -
_____

"Posterity! You will never know how much it cost the present generation to preserve your freedom! I hope you will make a good use of it."

--John Adams

_____
- -
_____
- -
_____

Famous Quotes of the Civil War

Directions: Read the famous quotes from the Civil War era and note the authors. Copy the quotes using proper cursive writing form.

> *"A house divided against itself cannot stand."*
>
> --Abraham Lincoln

> *"...there was one of two things I had a right to, liberty, or death; if I could not have one, I would have the other; ..."*
>
> --Harriet Tubman

> *"There can be no neutrals in this war; only patriots and traitors."*
>
> --Stephen Arnold Douglas

Name: _____ Date: _____

Notable Historical Quotes

Directions: Copy the quotes using proper cursive writing form.

> *"I feel safe in the midst of my enemies, for the truth is all powerful and will prevail."*
>
> --Sojourner Truth

_____

- -

_____

- -

_____

> *"From where the sun now stands, I will fight no more forever."*
>
> --Chief Joseph

_____

- -

_____

- -

> *"Be of good cheer, for sadness cannot heal the national wounds."*
>
> --Dorothea Dix

_____

- -

_____

- -

_____

Name: _____ Date: _____

Great Literature: *Jungle Book*

Jungle Book is a collection of stories by **Rudyard Kipling**. The book is about a young boy named Mowgli who survives in the jungle as a member of a wolf pack.

> "This is the law of the jungle, it's old and it's true as the sky. And the wolf that should keep it may prosper, but the wolf who will break it must die. For the strength of the pack is the wolf and the strength of the wolf is the pack."

Directions: Copy the excerpt from *Jungle Book* using proper cursive writing form. If you need more paper, use a copy of the practice paper.

Name: _____ Date: _____

Great Literature: *The Call of the Wild*

The Call of the Wild is a novel by Jack London. The book is about Buck, a dog that endures many hardships in his effort to survive in the wilds of Alaska.

> *But especially he loved to run in the dim twilight of the summer midnights, listening to the subdued and sleepy murmurs of the forest, reading signs and sounds as a man may read a book, and seeking for the mysterious something that called—called, waking or sleeping, at all times, for him to come.*

Directions: Copy the excerpt from *The Call of the Wild* using proper cursive writing form. If you need more paper, use a copy of the practice paper.

Name: _____ Date: _____

Great Literature: *Little Women*

Little Women is a novel by Louisa May Alcott. The book is about the lives of four sisters: Meg, Jo, Beth, and Amy March.

> *"I want to do something splendid...something heroic or wonderful that won't be forgotten after I'm dead. I don't know what, but I'm on the watch for it and mean to astonish you all someday."*

Directions: Copy the excerpt from *Little Women* using proper cursive writing form. If you need more paper, use a copy of the practice paper.

_____

- -

_____

- -

_____

- -

_____

- -

_____

- -

_____

- -

_____

- -

_____

- -

_____

- -

_____

Name: _____ Date: _____

Great Literature: *The Adventures of Tom Sawyer*

The Adventures of Tom Sawyer is a novel by Mark Twain. The book is about a mischievous, yet courageous and resourceful boy growing up along the Mississippi River.

> *When they reached the haunted house there was something so weird and grisly about the dead silence that reigned there under the baking sun, and something so depressing about the loneliness and desolation of the place, that they were afraid, for a moment, to venture in.*

Directions: Copy the excerpt from *The Adventures of Tom Sawyer* using proper cursive writing form. If you need more paper, use a copy of the practice paper.

Name: _____ Date: _____

Great Literature: *The Velveteen Rabbit*

The Velveteen Rabbit is a novel by Margery Williams. The story is about a stuffed rabbit that desires to become real.

"Generally, by the time you are Real, most of your hair has been loved off, and your eyes drop out and you get loose in the joints and very shabby. But these things don't matter at all, because once you are Real you can't be ugly, except to people who don't understand."

Directions: Copy the excerpt from *The Velveteen Rabbit* using cursive writing. If you need more paper, use a copy of the practice paper.

Name: _____   Date: _____

Proverbs

In 1733, Benjamin Franklin began the publication of *Poor Richard's Almanac*. The book was printed annually from 1732 to 1758. It included weather and agricultural predictions, charts of the moon's phases, and a series of proverbs.

Directions: Copy the proverbs from *Poor Richard's Almanac* using proper cursive writing form.

1. Honesty is the best policy.

2. Great haste makes great waste.

3. Whatever is begun in anger ends in shame.

4. 'Tis easier to prevent bad habits than to break them.

5. Early to bed and early to rise, makes a man healthy, wealthy, and wise.

Name: _____ Date: _____

Tongue Twisters

A **tongue twister** is a phrase or sentence that is hard to say fast, because of the sequence of nearly similar sounds used in the expressions.

Directions: Copy the tongue twister using proper cursive writing form.

1. She sells seashells by the seashore. The shells she sells are surely seashells.

2. Fuzzy Wuzzy was a bear. Fuzzy Wuzzy had no hair. Fuzzy Wuzzy wasn't very fuzzy, was he?

3. Peter Piper picked a peck of pickled peppers. How many pecks of pickled peppers did Peter Piper pick?

Name: _____ Date: _____

Pangram Challenge

A **pangram** is a sentence that contains all the letters of the alphabet. Pangrams are a great way to practice penmanship. The most well-known pangram is

"The quick brown fox jumps over a lazy dog."

Directions: Work with a partner to create a pangram. Use a thesaurus or dictionary if you need help. Follow the steps below.

Step 1: Create the shortest pangram possible using all the letters of the alphabet.
Step 2: The pangram must be a complete sentence and make sense.
Step 3: Write your pangram in cursive on the lines below.
Step 4: Trade your completed pangram with another team. Copy their pangram in cursive writing at the bottom of the page.

My Pangram

_____

- -

_____

- -

_____

- -

_____

- -

_____

Traded Pangram

_____

- -

_____

- -

_____

- -

_____

- -

_____

Name: _____ Date: _____

Quill Pen and Ink Signature

> The colonists used quill pens and ink to write letters and important documents. Quill pens were made from the wing feathers of geese, turkeys, and other large birds. Thomas Jefferson wrote the Declaration of Independence using a quill pen. The fifty-five members of the Continental Congress who signed the document used a quill pen. John Hancock, president of the Congress, was the first to sign.

Activity #1
Directions: View the Declaration of Independence and the signatures of the colonists who signed the document online at <https://catalog.archives.gov/id/1656604>. Notice John Hancock's signature. It is reported that he wrote his name in this large and flamboyant style so the "King could read it without his spectacles."

Activity #2
Directions: Add your signature to the Declaration of Independence and print a copy of the document online at <https://www.archives.gov/exhibits/charters/declaration_sign.html>.

Activity #3
Directions: Make your own quill pen and ink by following these steps.

Step 1: Soak a large feather (about 10 inches long) in warm soapy water for 15 minutes. Dry it with a paper towel.
Step 2: Cut off the bottom two inches of the tip with scissors. Cut at an angle. This is the point of the pen called the nib.
Step 3: Use a pin or toothpick to carefully clean out the center of the nib.
Step 4: Cut a small slit in the nib. This helps control the flow of ink.
Step 5: Make ink by crushing one cup of berries through a strainer into a glass jar. Add 1 teaspoon of vinegar and one teaspoon of salt. If the ink is too pale, add a drop of red or blue food coloring. **CAUTION:** Cover your work area with newspapers. Do not spill ink on your clothes. It may leave a permanent stain.
Step 6: To write, dip the nib into the ink. Press off the excess ink on a paper towel. Hold the quill at an angle and write with the tip. Repeat this step when your pen runs out of ink.
Step 7: Practice writing your name on a separate piece of paper with your quill pen until you are satisfied with the way it looks. Then write your signature in the box below.

Signature Box

President Lincoln's Letter to Mrs. Bixby

During the Civil War, President Abraham Lincoln wrote a letter to Mrs. Bixby using a quill pen. The original letter no longer exists. However, a copy was printed in a Boston newspaper a few days after being delivered to Mrs. Bixby. Although the letter is admired by many scholars as one of Lincoln's greatest writings, there is some controversy concerning whether Abraham Lincoln or one of his aides wrote the letter.

> Executive Mansion
> Washington, Nov 21, 1864
>
> To Mrs Bixby, Boston, Mass,
>
>   Dear Madam,
>
>   I have been shown in the files of the War Department a statement of the Adjutant General of Massachusetts that you are the mother of five sons who have died gloriously on the field of battle. I feel how weak and fruitless must be any word of mine which should attempt to beguile you from the grief of a loss so overwhelming. But I cannot refrain from tendering you the consolation that may be found in the thanks of the republic they died to save. I pray that our Heavenly Father may assuage the anguish of your bereavement, and leave you only the cherished memory of the loved and lost, and the solemn pride that must be yours to have laid so costly a sacrifice upon the altar of freedom.
>
>   Yours very sincerely and respectfully,
>
>   A. Lincoln

Lincoln, Abraham. *[The Celebrated 'Bixby' letter. Facsimile]*. 1864. Manuscript/Mixed Material. Retrieved from the Library of Congress, <https://www.log.gov/item/scsm000360/>.

Name: _____ Date: _____

President Lincoln's Letter to Mrs. Bixby (cont.)

Directions: It is important to be able to write in cursive, but it is also important to be able to read cursive writing. Read Lincoln's letter to Mrs. Bixby. Answer the questions in complete sentences using cursive writing.

1. Where and when was the letter written?

_____

_____

_____

2. How many sons of Mrs. Bixby died in the war?

_____

3. What was Lincoln's purpose for writing the letter?

_____

_____

_____

4. Lincoln wrote thousands of documents, and his handwriting is well known. What tip would you give the president for improving his cursive penmanship?

_____

_____

_____

_____

Write to a Pen Pal

It is exciting to visit the mailbox and find a thick envelope inside with your name carefully written on the outside. There is something special about opening the envelope and finding a letter especially written for you. A pen pal is someone with whom you can exchange letters. Having a pen pal is a great way to make a new friend while learning about another school, town, state, or country.

Pen Pal Toolkit

- loose-leaf notebook paper or nice stationery
- fountain pen or ball point pen (blue or black ink)
- envelope
- stamps

Writing a Great Letter

- **Share Information About yourself:** Your pen pal will want to know all about you and your interests. Write about a pet, your hobbies, sports programs or school clubs you are involved with, what you did during the week, what you love to eat, or your favorite school subject, book, movie, or video game.
- **Ask Questions:** Think of pen pal writing as conversation on paper. It is important to tell about yourself but also to ask questions about your pen pal. It shows your new friend that you are interested in his or her life and what they have to say.
- **Be Creative:** Personalize your letter by including a "tuck-in" such as a drawing, school picture, special sticker, or trading card.

Address the Envelope Correctly

Addressing the envelope correctly is important. If your letter isn't properly addressed, your pen pal will probably not get the letter. There are three parts to correctly addressing an envelope: return address, delivery address, and stamp.

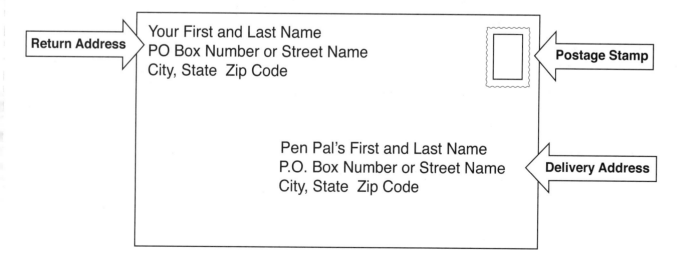

Parts of a Pen Pal Letter

When you write to your pen pal, you will be using the friendly letter format. A friendly letter includes several parts: heading, greeting, body, closing, and signature.

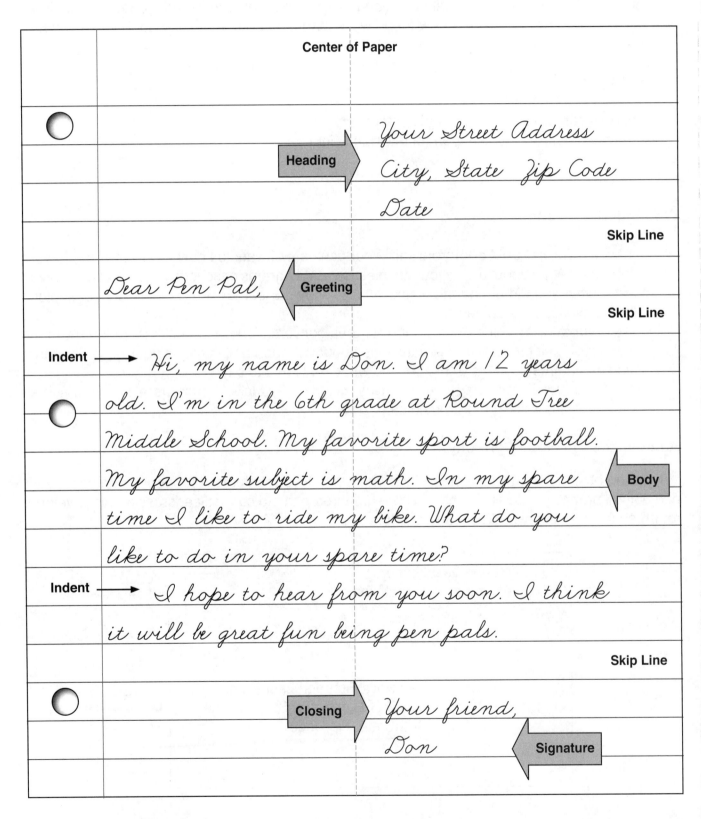